I0171591

THE BATTLED CHRISTIAN, DEAD AT THE CROSS:

THE JOURNEY OF THE SUICIDAL WOMAN OF GOD

JT CONSULTING LLC

New York, New York

Unless otherwise indicated, all Scripture quotations are taken from the Holy Bible, New Living Translation, copyright © 1996, 2004, 2007 by Tyndale House Foundation. Used by permission of Tyndale House Publishers, Inc., Carol Stream, Illinois 60188. Used by permission. All rights reserved.

Published by:
Marisa McClinton
JT Consulting
New York, New York
www.Blessedbella82@gmail.com

Copyright © 2014
Marisa McClinton

All rights reserved. No part of this book may be reproduced or transmitted in any form or any matter, electronic of mechanical, including photocopying, recording or by any information storage and retrieval system, without permission in writing from author/publisher/ Please direct all inquiries to blessedbella82@gmail.com.

ISBN 13-9780615946115

Printed in the United States of America

This book is dedicated to the all-powerful and forever gracious Lord Jesus Christ, for without him I would have accomplished nothing.

TABLE OF CONTENTS

Authors Note

Depression is an occurrence that many struggle through on a daily basis. I struggled with it since I was a teenager and still feel the effects in my adulthood. My purpose for this book is to show those who are also suffering the effects, that what we go through isn't shameful or dishonorable to God. There are many trials in this life and while many of us process some of them as learning experiences; there are others who have become afraid and held back in their daily walk because of them. I have suffered many traumatic and many hurtful experiences and while they have stunted my growth at times, I was able to, ultimately, be saved by the love and grace of the kingdom. I felt a desperate need to be free and to accept all that God had purposed for me. When I encourage others who are going through difficult times, I remind them that when God made them, he wasn't mistaken about the call he put on his/ her walk, hence why the enemy encourages the amount of trials he does. I learned that not all my troubles were from the enemy, but were results of destructive behaviors and mindsets brought about from the bondage of my inability to let go and trust God to heal the hurts and afflictions of those who hurt me. My afflictions grew into hindrances which snowballed into manifestations of greater obstacles. My goal with this book is to encourage those who are struggling to see that there is hope for what they are feeling and going through and that what they may be experiencing does have a source and a name. While the world may not understand all that goes into the diagnosis of depression and the causes of suicide; there is hope that there is a creator that is willing and able to reveal to us our pain and assist us through the valley towards wholeness and healing. With surrender and trust, there is healing, freedom, and joy. I urge you, reader, to trust the process, believe in yourself, and do not lose hope because you have a purpose, you have meaning, and you have the strength to make it through this storm. And if you are reading this to assist somebody else, please do not lose patience with them. Be brave for his or her sake and trust God with your words and your efforts; because if it wasn't for the people who tarried with me night and day, these words would have never been born. Remember, with God, ALL things are possible; he's able.

CHAPTER ONE
Where I end and God begins

Proverbs 3:5-6
New Living Translation (NLT)
[5] Trust in the Lord with all your heart;
do not depend on your own understanding.
[6] Seek his will in all you do,
and he will show you which path to take.

There was me, the small town girl, who grew up in such a small world that even I couldn't figure out why I was feeling the way I was feeling. A child isn't born depressed, a child is born uninhibited of pain and of thought; it's the world that casts down the innocence of a child with its expectations and its empty promises of a life of promise and excellence. My first season of conscience thought of depression came with my teenage years. The doctors called it a "chemical imbalance" but to me, it was a dark room of thoughts, emotions, and questions as to why I was alone in a world full of people. I asked myself "how could a car drive past me and not see me standing here?" I didn't understand what part of this dark season was meant for my good until I reached the ripe age of 30. Could you imagine being 16 years old and having no clue that I wouldn't understand what is going on with me until I was 30 years old? I look back on that girl and feel so much remorse for her because she would have to suffer and pang for the next 14 years. When I read the Bible, I saw many people suffer and cry out to the Lord for decades, centuries and even millenniums; but the only issue is, I wasn't a girl who was crying out to God, at least I didn't think I was.

An excerpt from my book *"The Suicidal Christian: The battle is the mind"*
    "As searing pain ran through my body I looked around and seen that there was nobody there to help me. I wanted to scream in pain but my environment wouldn't let me. I felt like I was drowning in my soul and choking on my own spirit. The stench of failure surrounded me as I remembered all of the rotten things I have done since I was an infant. I thought of my father and how the only thing he could have done to tolerate me was leave and never look back. I've seen my mother and remembered every single time I looked into her eyes and seen nothing. The fear of a death so dishonorable to God that I would be held in a special section of hell for all eternity, but a death that seemed to be the only recourse in the face of a storm so painful that only Jesus knew what it felt like. Persecution, dishonesty, shame, embarrassment, all the feelings of a life that never went the path God ordained it to. Questions with no answers and visions with no sound seemed to be my reality. The water that filled my lungs tasted of sulfur and brine. My eyes burned with tears of rocks and my ear rang of all the mistakes I have ever made. Was this my end? Have I been fooling myself the entire time to think that God would actually want to save me? Petty thoughts such as this ran across my forehead, but yet there I stood on the edge of the bridge with nothing but hell burning below me. Where is God? A fair question to ask when you have a noose around your neck and you're ready to kick the chair. So to continue to be fair, I currently don't have an answer for that question. Let's first examine the spirit of suicide and depression before we try to determine how to defeat it.

Depression, to depress holds down, bring low, hold back, and apply pressure too and the list of descriptions go on for decades. When a person falls into a depression, they often feel sad, "down in the dumps", maybe angry, anxious, afraid, hopeless and bound. Depression is a "depress" in a persons' emotional state, which can be accompanied with physical symptoms and reactions. Depression has a wide range of causes and symptoms from genetic to situational. The enemy uses depression to incapacitate people and keep them distracted from serving their ultimate purpose. While the enemy is attempting to isolate and manipulate the person from people who can protect them, he can also surround the person with people he is using to further catapult them into a depressed state. One of my biggest issues is the phrase "don't rely on man, man will always fail you" a solid truth and an ongoing theme in the word of God. But Lord, I say, you have put me dead smack in the middle of a planet with millions upon millions of those people that I am not supposed to rely on. Lord, these people that I am not supposed to rely on are in my face all day every day, so what am I supposed to do? "Lord show me someone other than Jesus who keeps their eyes on you 24-7 and maybe I'll feel a little bit better"...still waiting. What is it about ending your life that seems to ease the pain that life brings? A question I have thought about for years and even more in the past few months. As a Christian, I was raised to know about heaven and hell. It's no surprise the kind of place hell is and what goes there, while no one really has a clear picture of exactly what the sights and sounds consist of, saved and unsaved alike can agree that it's no place for anyone to desire to be. But here's the thing, as a Christian, I had a close encounter with the things of God, his word and his enemy, so why would the thought of ending my life even enter my mind? Again a question I have asked for years. The devil or the "enemy" as we like to call him has a mission to destroy; especially those who are chosen by God to fulfill a specific purpose for the kingdom of righteousness and against the kingdom of darkness. The devil doesn't like me or any other Christian Brother or sister of mine. From the womb I have been a threat to the devil. He's been throwing curve balls at me since I could remember my first memory. Yet, everything changed when I gave my life to the Lord. Ready to commit the ultimate sin, Gods power was able to grab my attention long enough to cancel the assignment of hell and redeem my spiritual self. So there I am saved and on the road to sanctification and yes the devil was madder than, well hell. Throughout my walk in previous years, I grew and grew more on fire for the things of the kingdom. Secrets were exposed to me and visions were cast upon my head. The Lord worked through me and for me in every area of my life. I didn't and I don't have it all but when you measure "all" not in worldly attributes but in spiritual treasures, then you can call me wealthy. I am no way shape or form anywhere near to where I am required to be but I can look back and realize that God has carried far from where I left those worldly shoes. So the Lord continued to reveal things to me and teach me about the things of the kingdom and I invited it with open arms. I've seen things that were inviting and I've seen things that simply destroyed my sleep patterns, but I've vowed to go through anything he could throw at me for the sake of working for the Lord. The one thing that I noticed a lot with the body of Christ and the "body of Christ" is that there is a large part in this red sea. The visual that is given of when Moses parted the sea to escape the soldiers show a large-scale ocean- like river that was as deep as it was wide. When the staff hit the ground, the water raised up to the sky clearing a path for Moses and the Israelites giving them a safe method of escape. This same type of imagery can be used for the parting of the churches "red sea". Let's examine myself for a moment; there are times when it is easy to praise God because everything is roses and unicorns. The kids are honor roll students, the spouse is doing dishes, and the checkbook is more balanced than the tires on your car. Then there's the times when either the devil gets sick of the smell of all those roses or the Lord thinks that you are getting too comfortable on that unicorn and all that water comes crashing back down to earth. Now don't get me wrong, I know that nobody promised me that a saved life is a perfect, *flawless, tear less life; but I regretted to remember that for one with a different level comes a different devil. Two, when you nag God enough he might just give it to you to show you exactly why he didn't give it to you yet. Finally. It's the season for conditioning and training. Regardless of the reason for the season, these moments of pressure washing, tightening, shifting, moving, suffocating, cleansing, gutting and cutting can be difficult for some and unbearable to others. There have been "tests" and "trials" that I have been through that seemed like they were just pricks by the smallest needle, but then once those quickly passed, the real storm came and knocked my ship all over the bay. Again, there were some storms that I went into with mountain moving strength and I endured like a true, anointed woman of God; so well that I could see thee smile on Gods face in the morning sky. The confidence flowed through me like the blood in my veins, and the true power of God burst out of my mouth as strong and gentle as the Holy Ghost filled the church of Acts on the day of Pentecost. I look back on some of those crowing moments and celebrate a bittersweet victory. As I write this I feel the joy of knowing that my anointing was never an illusion, but then I huddle in shame as to the weakness I feel as I type these words. Whether I call myself a prophet or not, I cannot deny the discernment I had for the approaching of this very storm. The smells, the sights, the thoughts, the feelings, the anger, the shame, the exhaustion and the confusion that I feel were all there in my spirit moments before it approached; almost like seeing the bolts of lightning off in the distance accompanied by the wall of rain just over the mountain tops, but with the absence of the thunder that completes the vision of the true storm of the century. The best part is that I realize it while I write about it. A few weeks ago I felt an unsettling in my spirit. I began to see those close to me back off slowly, I began to feel the urge to dispose of loose ends and to cleanse myself of foolishness. I felt my body tightening up like it was trying to protect its core from attack. Many forensic scientists say that when the body is under attack or feel threatened, it will go into automatic defense mode and begin to protect its core. For instance, the body will curl up in the fetal position when it is being beaten to protect the vital organs within the mid sections such as the lungs, heart, intestines, and even tuck the head to protect the face and head. The same as the physical body, the spiritual body will begin to sense an attack and immediately go into protection mode. I can say that I can't even complain or get upset because this type of closeness and attachment to the things of the spirit realm is what I desired and what I spent many nights praying for; so the lesson here is be aware and be careful of what you pray for. So at this point in my journey, I am hear battling one the largest demons I have ever faced in my life and I am doing it with absolutely no power at all."*

My first book, "*The Suicidal Christian*" was written during a time of misunderstanding; believe it or not the book was actually written three years before it was actually published. I look at it and was given the revelation as to how a person could write a book to help someone else when they themselves was still under the thumb of confusions and misguidances. You'll be surprised as to how many people can be awakened by the sleep of another person. I call it sleep because I was in a perpetual deep sleep of depression. I was weighed down by the dark, dismal underbrush of a life of confusion, fear, suicide, and disgust. I embarrassed myself any chance I got and I searched for acceptance through sex, lust, drugs, alcohol, and utter sinful behavior. Unlike the typical revelation, it didn't take death to get me on my knees to God, it couldn't take death because death wasn't a part of my plan at the time. See when God has a plan for someone's life, not even death can come to claim their name. God is the creator of the beginning and the end of a person, despite what may happen in between those occurrences, the Lord himself is the one who is calling all the shots. I, myself is proof of that age old truth.

The Battled Christian

At 16 years old, I was making decisions that a grown adult couldn't even make. I couldn't find the light switch for my brain. Every thought was dark and every breath I took was hopeless. I couldn't understand why I was born alone, why I didn't have the popularity of my friends at school, why I didn't have a boyfriend, why I didn't have rich parents, why I didn't have God, why I didn't have a purpose, why I even existed. Of course I look back on that season and see how I was blinded by the cloud of depression, but at the time I couldn't feel that deception. In my fear and delusion, I reached out for solutions instead of Gods conclusion. I wanted to go away, I wanted to run, but to where? I wanted to hide from myself and my thoughts but I couldn't go with it following me. my dreams were my solace, my dreams were my place of escape, in my dreams my life was amazing, my life made sense and my life had purpose; but it was the alarm going off that made my death even more logical. Being awake was the hardest part of my existence because it was during the day that my proof of despair was hanging on my arm like a bracelet of thorns. I was afraid of my own shadow, I was angry at the sun. I looked around at all the happy people and hated them for being content with this thing called "life"; I wanted them to see my pain and feel it, I wanted them to be haunted by it and feel bad for being so happy. I was miserable and wanted everyone to know about it. I couldn't feel my feet and I could get rid of my brain; it was utter torture being me, least that's what I thought.

My first attempt at summoning death came as a teenager. I wanted to end the pain I was suffering the only way I knew how and the only way I could find and that was suicide. I have the faintest memory of it, but I remember being in the hospital and being asked 'why?' how could I answer such a trivial question? How that could make and sense to a person who just swallowed a lifetime worth of pills hoping to not wake up. "What kind of madness is this?" I asked myself in utter confusion. While they admitted me to the psychiatric ward, I wondered what kind of "help" these people who have no idea what sadness is, can offer a useless girl such as me. I wondered what their motivation was and why they even existed; such a complex thought for such a little girl. See the enemy will come in like a flood, when he has his assignment to destroy you, he will flood your mind with thoughts that have no logical bearing on the rotation of the earth, but if you are weak in Christ and weak in spirit than those thoughts will consume you and drown you in their illogic. At the time, I didn't know the difference between life and death. Purpose and hope meant nothing to me because I couldn't see myself as anything more than the mistake of the century. I was lost within myself and bruised from the fight of my mind. After a few days in this "ward" I met people, kids, and teenagers with serious problems. I mean, I thought I had issues, but these kids had some real emotionally deficiencies. Then it hit me one day in group that I wasn't like these people. I wasn't a troubled youth that hated her parents, I wasn't a runaway, I wasn't on drugs and I wasn't refusing to go to school; I was sad, I was tired, I was confused, I was sick. It was here that I discovered the beginning of what would be 14 years of a journey towards purpose and hope. The hospital sent me home a month later with a bag of more pills and an appointment to see a therapist. Well I quickly realized that even the hospital couldn't figure out my issue and their only solution was to medicate me enough to forget why I was sad. A scientific solution to a spiritual problem. I was a zombie, not a fixed zombie, but a broken zombie. I was highly medicated but still lost; some would say that it was because I didn't have God but when I look back on that season, God was truly there in that dark room with me. There isn't any other reason why a person could take as many pills as I did and wake up like nothing had happened. This type of occurrence happened several different times over the course of my 14 year journey and each time proved that God himself has his hands on the righteous; even the righteous that didn't know they were meant to be righteous. The devil can have you questioning your own existence, he can have you looking at the lack of your life and convincing you that you are at the worst of your life. He can put a distorted mirror in front of your face and tell you that the face you see is how the world sees you. There were many nights when I sat with God and was looking at myself through the eyes of hell.

The Battled Christian

"*Today I felt the entire universe on my shoulders so I went for a run. I ran, sometimes fast with a sprint and other times slow with a hop; either way, I was running. I wasn't sure if I was running from something or if I was running to someone. I felt the defeat of my own actions rise up in my gut like a bad case of heart burn. I sat in my car and I heard the devil tell me to drive as fast as I could into that tree across the parking lot. To get back on the road towards my house and accelerate until I could no longer feel the safety of my brake pedals, to continue to drive straight until the road bent and go nose first into the pine in my neighbor's lawn. What would that prove? Who would that destroy? My death... who would care and who would be there to identify my remains, if any? A dark thought from the mind of a Christian woman who doesn't understand why the pressures of the world are standing on the top of my head. A woman who is beautiful in the eyes of many and smart in the eyes of her children. A woman who is waiting for her Boaz and striving toward her father in excellence. A woman misunderstood, mistreated, and misguided. A woman who the world brought up to ignore. A woman who the world taught how to hate herself and how to hate others. A woman of pain. Like Job who was the man of anguish in the Bible, Jabez who was born as the symbol of pain to his family. I am their sister, a woman of hurt and un-forgiveness. A woman who is struggling even today with her very will to live. The woman who is the suicidal Christian. Why? She asks? Why doesn't anyone pay any attention to her? Why she is only looked upon as a sex object. Why doesn't her mother love her and why doesn't her father care? Why doesn't the church let her speak and why doesn't the devil just leave her alone? Why is she the object of so much in her own mind? Why is she stuck on the unseen when the lord reveals so much? Why is she here when she can only regret her own existence?*"

The enemy is free to run rampant in our minds, if we allow him too.

Psalm 91:2
New Living Translation (NLT)
[2] This I declare about the Lord:
He alone is my refuge, my place of safety;
he is my God, and I trust him.

CHAPTER TWO
Know your enemy: The demon part II

John 10:10

New Living Translation (NLT)

[10] The thief's purpose is to steal and kill and destroy. My purpose is to give them a rich and satisfying life.

From my previous book, *"The Suicidal Christian: the battle is the mind"* I go into detail about the spirit of depression and suicide. Unknown to most, the symptoms of depression are inclinations of spiritual upheaval.

<u>Depression symptoms include</u>:

*not limited too but may include

- Feelings of sadness or unhappiness
- Irritability or frustration, even over small matters
- Loss of interest or pleasure in normal activities
- Reduced sex drive
- Insomnia or excessive sleeping
- Changes in appetite — depression often causes decreased appetite and weight loss, but in some people it causes increased cravings for food and weight gain
- Agitation or restlessness — for example, pacing, hand-wringing or an inability to sit still
- Irritability or angry outbursts
- Slowed thinking, speaking or body movements
- Indecisiveness, distractibility and decreased concentration
- Fatigue, tiredness and loss of energy — even small tasks may seem to require a lot of effort
- Feelings of worthlessness or guilt, fixating on past failures or blaming yourself when things aren't going right
- Trouble thinking, concentrating, making decisions and remembering things
- Frequent thoughts of death, dying or suicide

- Crying spells for no apparent reason
- Unexplained physical problems, such as back pain or headaches

(Mayo Clinic, n.d., p. 1)

Demonic influence Symptoms:

*not limited too but may include

- Thinking thoughts which are "not like you" or which "seem to come from somewhere else" or which "come out of the blue".
- Sudden depression. Sometimes the depression is severe, sometimes it is very subtle.
- Feeling like suicide, like life is not worth living or wondering why you are here.
- Having severe arguments with your spouse or friends.
- Feelings of hopelessness.
- Feeling like someone or something else is controlling you. You may feel controlled all the time or only some of the time.
- Feeling like someone or something is pressuring you to do certain acts.
- Feeling something touch you, scratch you, or otherwise attack you.
- Hearing one or multiple voices in your head that are negative, persuasive, or commanding you to do something. For example, hearing a voice persuade you that a certain friend should be avoided, or asking you to let them "in" to your life in some way.
- Deep personality changes. For example, someone stays at home all the time when they used to be very gregarious.
- Creepy feelings.
- An area of your house or your neighborhood which feels negative or oppressive.
- Any kind of phenomena. For example, scratching sounds, things falling off walls or shelves, religious or spiritual items being moved or changed.
- Feeling attacked when others do not see or experience anything. Sometimes this feeling of being attacked may come with physical pain that is medically inexplicable. Usually it will come with psychological pain of some sort – terror or anguish for example.

- An aversion to prayer or an inability to pray.

- Being unable to stand any contact with religious or spiritual items. For example, sudden strong aversion to going into a church or temple, aversion to being touched by a crucifix, and so on.("SYMPTOMS OF DEMONIC ATTACK & POSSESSION | Demon Slayer", n.d., p. 1)

Within these two vivid descriptions, there are some similarities and commonalities. The enemy's purpose is to steal, kill and destroy; which could be anything ranging from emotions, physical, mental stability, and spiritual awareness. The enemy is girded with lies and confusion, in fact he is the author of lies and confusion. In my own personal season, I was experiencing a hell that I had never knew existed. I was terrified and cast down by a force that was beyond my control. I was in a constant motion of swinging at the wind and boxing with the air. I was lost in the battle of evil. Even when I did receive Christ into my life once again, I still found myself in the perpetual war with getting back my sanity. I analyzed the demon of suicide in my first book, but I want to take it a step further.

An excerpt from my book *"The Suicidal Christian: the battle is the mind"*

"The demon of suicide has been in my family and on my back for years, but for the most part a little prayer and a little oil helps me to weather the long nights; but God! This night is no ordinary night. I noticed that the people I normally broke bread with were beginning to back away slowly. I have looked around and seen that there was no body left for me to go to and listen to me. There was nobody there to understand and nobody there to discern me. I felt betrayed even though I knew the Lord's word about how I must seek his face only and that my only idol should be him. Truthfully, that is fine but Lord you put me on a planet with other people by yet there is not one to understand what is going on with me. Okay I get it, "how can a worldly being understand a spiritual event?" good question Lord, so then tell me how am I supposed to get an army together if you have removed all of my recruits? I think it's a bit hilarious how I am sitting here going back and forth with God of all people about these details. So in the back of my mind, all I hear are the saints talking all those Sundays about trusting God with all your being and even myself speaking to others about complete and utter surrender. So, if I know so much about the blue prints, then why can't I still build this house?? Okay Lord I am listening, but first you have to hear me out. Imagine the sound of

the Lord giggling in the back of your mind when you tell him something like that. So anyway, here I am, hurt betrayed, sad, ashamed, exhausted, angry, disappointed, afraid, nervous, hopeless, and just plain over it. I'm sitting here right now without a friend in the world, battling the suicide demon with my left hand, trying to forgive with the right hand, typing this book with the left side of my brain while trying to let go of the pain with my right. Just imagine the battle that I am going through; I'm trying to keep my natural eyes open while trying to close my spiritual eyes to the truth. Oh Lord can you see my turmoil. I have been betrayed by my family, been abused by my church family, laughed at by my friends, persecuted at my job, rode like a dog by my kids, and even my own bed won't let me get peace. Two weeks this has been going on and you would think that when I saw this storm coming that I would of went to the tore and got my rations but no I was comfortable on my unicorn. I thought the same anointing that carried me through the other storms would definitely carry me through this tornado; insert dramatic laugh here. So here I stand, alone in the natural but surrounded by the entire kingdom of heaven in the spirit, but I have been chilling at this pity party for so long that I can't even get myself up long enough to pray for some help. The devil is laughing behind my right shoulder because he thinks he got me pinned with a bottle of pills in my hand but neither one of us can figure out how a person can take so many pills and still wake up the next day. Okay so it's been confirmed, the Lord has more for me than just the bottom of an empty pill bottle, fantastic, BUT how am I supposed to continue like this? The saints say to pray, but what is prayer when every time you look in the mirror you see the demon that is whispering in your ear about all these things going wrong? What is prayer to the person who is to the point of having over 35 pills in their mouth and no one around to tell them to spit them out? I'm sorry Lord but honestly what is prayer when you're so weak that all you can think about despite all the truth you know is to take the life that was already paid for? The Lord says that this life, my life is not my own. I do not have the authority to do what I feel like with it nor do I have the authority to take it or leave it whenever I wish. So there's the catch 22. I am a Christian who loves the Lord with all of her being; can praise, worship, fast, pray, speak in tongues, dance, sing, and speak with authority and I am at the lowest point of my Christian walk and there is nothing I can do about it. I look in the spirit and I see rows and rows of faces standing all around me. They all face me and they all glow with the peace and protection of the kingdom. I hear the Lord say that this is my army but I have the power to control them and they cannot move until I am ready to instruct them to go forth. "So Lord what you are saying is that you removed all of my earthly and worldly presence and surrounded my spirit with the biggest and most powerful army of the kingdom but they will not move until I instruct them too? Okay Lord well that's not fair because I am not done with my pity party yet!" And there he goes laughing again. But "Lord I am serious, these people hurt me! They talked about me and lied on me at my job, and counted me out, and jumped over me and pushed me down and ignored me and didn't even bother to get to know me before they judged me. They prayed against me and gossiped about me. They ignored your word flowing out of me, they laughed at me when I praise you and they kicked me when I was down. Lord they even read my book and criticized it!! Lord how could you sit there and see all of this and not do anything?? My feelings are hurt, my spirit is hurt and I feel like I have been living a lie, like I've been lied to and cheated. Lord you know how I grew up so why do you let them sleep at night while I suffer with what they did to me?? And please don't tell me how they did the same to Jesus because I am so tired of hearing about that".

To compare and contrast this portion of my life, I was fighting both with and without consciously knowing of Gods power and Gods might. This was the first occurrence of the enemies' show of assignment he had in my entire life and this was also the first revelation of Gods power since I realized how the pull of depression and suicide was impacting my life.

The spirit of depression can be seen through the spirit of heaviness. The devil comes to "depress" our ability to push towards fulfilling the will of the kingdom while "suppressing" our ability to realize and consciously accept Gods love and devotion to our well – being. He uses suicide as a way to get us to separate ourselves from God being that he doesn't have the power to kill us himself. He uses trickery and deceit to convince us that hope is lost, that God has left, and that we have nothing else to live for. He uses our own ears against us and plants seeds of doubt in God during times of tribulations and difficulty. He will speak a gaggle of lies and implant the spirit of heaviness over us to convince us that we cannot and will not find a way out of this so called valley of death but in Psalms 23 David spoke that although he walked through the valley of death, he will fear any evil. The same evil that David was facing during his time of trial is the same evil released upon us when we suffer with the cloud of depression. Depression has been looked upon in many different ways over the course of history; from a mental break down to a spiritual possession. Currently, there are many forms of treatment and diagnosis for what society called "depressive disorder". there comes a period in a persons depressed state that they can no longer just treat the symptoms but discover and destroy the root of this season. While there are many medical reasons for the depressed state that some may experience, God has shown us that he, alone, has created the beginning and the end and he alone knows the depths and recoveries of the very discrepancies that have plagued his people. "The source of depression in our lives is most likely a spiritual one; we try to obey Our Lord YAHUSHUA, Satan sends his demon(s) to torment us and get us to disobey. The Bible says that we have a Spirit of Power, Faith, Love and a Sound mind, The Holy Spirit. The evil spirit of depression that attaches itself to us directly attacks these fruits of the Holy Spirit.

The evil spirit shapes Power into weakness, great fatigue, and exhaustion of body, mind and spirit – no strength, no energy, no desire to do anything for the Lord YAHUSHUA The evil spirit shapes Faith into fear, unbelief, doubts, worries, fears – no hope, no confidence, no rest, no stability, no peace

The evil spirit shapes Love into selfishness, jealousy through insecurity, easily offended, little patience – a hard time to fellowship with brothers and sisters in YAHUSHUA, not really able to serve or minister unto others in any kind of way The evil spirit shapes the Sound Mind into a sinful mind no captivity of thoughts for the Lord YAHUSHUA - with all the further consequences of sinful thoughts and acting without Wisdom or Understanding." (Spiritual warfare, 2013)

The Battled Christian

The greatest thrill for the enemy is to stifle the work of the Holy Spirit and his greatest assignment is to attack our minds with lies and focus on our shortcomings. I know every time I was struggling with my joy, fighting against death, and depressed in my body I knew that it started with the thoughts within my mind that ultimately manifested into the encouragement of the spirit of heaviness. I felt it in my body and I felt it in my mind. I felt a sense of numbing in the mind; like I was chained to a chair in a movie theatre watching a replay of all the horrible things that have and could have happened in my life. I couldn't move and before I knew it those thoughts turned into a physical pain that exhausted my body, caused excessive migraines, made my joints and my bones hurt uncontrollably, and left me paralyzed with fear and agony. My spirit would jump and dance wildly inside of me because it knew the voice of God and it knew the attack that I was under, but my flesh wouldn't or couldn't comply. It was in this that I learned that the flesh was a weak entity; it has no self-control and it has no strength to withstand an inkling of criticism or failure, hence why the enemy uses those first when approaching a person he's assigned to destroy. It lies in our past mistakes and pitfalls, the failures of our youth and the mistakes of our ignorance is what fuels the enemy's attack against our mind. It takes but a mere reminder of something we have done wrong and then before we know it we are face down in our pillow crying out to a God that our flesh isn't even convinced anymore cares about us or even hears us. I've had stints of sitting on a ledge of bridge with a voice in ear telling me to jump because all that I thought was golden was simply gone and all that I thought I knew about God was a mere lie of the people who never cared about me anyway. I mean look at what I just said, a mouthful of lies that was manifested by the author of lies; but this was the very thought that entered my mind that set the stage of suicide in my head. It began with the mind and the battle within. The battle begins with the mind, because the mind knows what it sees. The mind sees the bills not paid, the kids not eating, the job going nowhere, the marriage breaking up, the friends leaving, and the car breaking down; while the spirit sees the God of mercy and miracles, hears the voice of the holy spirits promises, and feels the presences of the kingdom of the most high. The battle is the conflict between good and evil; the flesh being evilly controlled and the spirit pointed towards God and shaped by God being dynamically triumphant. The turning point came when I learned the lesson of wrestling not with flesh and blood but with principalities. I learned that the demon that I was fighting was not my fleshly self and the mistakes I have made and the shortcomings of my existence but with the principality of evil that was assigned to stop me from reaching the God that he already knows has a weapon of mass destruction to his dark, dismal kingdom. See, the devil knows who you are in Christ, the only issue is, and you don't! I had no idea who I was in Christ, I had no clue what I was made for and it was in that lack of wisdom that the enemy was able to convince me that I had no purpose and no reason to keep fighting a day longer. I was misinformed and miscommunicated by my own self and the enemy used that to his advantage.

The greatest lesson for me to learn as a suicidal young woman was to learn my enemy and learn his ways, then begin my battle. Before I knew the enemy, I was swinging in the dark with a sharpened sword. The difference now is that I know my enemy so I am able to see my enemy and use the weapons God gave me more effectively and confidently.

CHAPTER THREE
The daily battle

Job 7:15-16

New Living Translation (NLT)

[15] I would rather be strangled—

rather die than suffer like this.

[16] I hate my life and don't want to go on living.

Oh, leave me alone for my few remaining days.

In my thirty years of existence I have seen many professionals attempt to erect many solutions to the mental health deficiencies of this society with a large amount of failure; I believe this is due to the fact that the big picture is focused on more than the daily battle. It takes a daily compilation of thoughts, emotions, occurrences, and feelings that contribute to the larger picture of what a person is experiencing when they are battling with suicidal thoughts and depression.

1 Corinthians 10:13

New Living Translation (NLT)

[13] The temptations in your life are no different from what others experience. And God is faithful. He will not allow the temptation to be more than you can stand. When you are tempted, he will show you a way out so that you can endure.

My daily battle consisted of the fears and the misunderstandings of the world. A world that I put to high regard of my feelings like I did it; I couldn't understand why the world would label and forget someone who didn't fit in with them. I recently reached out to God for help. After the breakup of what I thought was the one God had for me, I found that a lifetime worth of rejection and fear came flooding back. I didn't understand why this kept happening to me. Why I experienced more tears than joy and more pain than happiness. I didn't understand why I lived in the valley of abandonment. Why I was forced to live a life of loss and complete loneliness.

I didn't understand what was so wrong with me that everyone I loved and cared for left me as quick as they came. Emotions I lived with; hurt and fear. I hear on a daily basis how letting go is the remedy to the soul; but how can I let go of what made me into what I am today? How can I walk away from the very thing that defines me? Like Jabez, named and born in pain, the definition of pain. Daily I smell the stench of mistakes, I hear the echoes of my words and see the reflections of my short comings. It's a daily walk of defeat and a daily race on the treadmill of failure. I've grown exceptionally weary of my own strength and profoundly distrusting of my own instincts. I've watched myself sow evil into my life and defeat into my day. I would praise the Lord with my mouth and fear life with my head. I would watch the Lord bless me and turn and ask him why he wasted this on me. I asked him why I was born and why I was meant to live for so long. I wondered what was in store for such a retch like me. I suffered and endured the pain and ripping apart of the vultures of my past; daily. Every day was a stretch; from finding the will to get out of bed, to finding the will to finish the day. I was in battle for my life. While I knew that the Lord was fighting the battle for me, my body would react to the spiritual blows. I never was able to comprehend the fact that all I had to do was stand there and hold faith that Yeshua was fighting for me, that his strength is more than enough and that his battle cry is much louder than mine could ever be. The truth of the matter is that depression, suicide, and warfare is a daily battle that can either be seen or be hidden in the daily dreck of our daily activities.

An excerpt from my previous book *"The Suicidal Christian: The battle is the mind"*;

THE BRIDGE

A WOMAN JUMPED TO HER DEATH THURSDAY NIGHT. I DIDNT KNOW HER BUT I FEEL HORRIBLE I COULDN'T SAVE HER. WHEN I WAS CROSSING THE BRIDGE AFTER WORK I SEEN A CAR PARKED ON THE SIDE OF THE ROAD WITH ITS HAZARDS ON; NO ONE IN IT OR AROUND IT. I THINK I WAS THE ONLY ONE WHO NOTICED IT BUT I IMMEDIATELY FELT SOMETHNG WAS WRONG...I DIDNT KNOW WHY BUT I WAS URGED TO LOOK AT THE SIDES OF THE BRIDGE FOR A PERSON...I DIDNT KNOW WHAT KIND OF PERSON ALL I KNEW WAS THAT I WAS LOOKING FOR ANYONE WALKING, STANDING OR RUNNING ON THE BRIDGE...I DIDNT SEE

ANYONE BUT I SWORE TO MYSELF THE MINUTE I DID I WAS GONNA STOP THE CAR AND RUN AFTER THEM...I CROSSED THE ENTIRE BRIDGE AND DIDN'T SEE ANYONE...I STILL COULDNT SHAKE THE FEELNG THAT SOMTHING WAS WRONG...I DIDNT SLEEP THAT NIGHT I JUST PRAYED. THE NEXT DAY WAS THE DAY FROM HELL FOR ME, STRESSED OUT AND AT THE END OF MY ROPE, I WAS LOSING MY MIND.THE DEVIL WAS ON MY BACK AND HE WAS HOLDNG ON TIGHT.I WAS BURIED NECK DEEP IN DESPAIR, AFTER WORK ALL I COULD DO WAS RUN TO THE CHURCH FOR SANCTUARY AND I DIDNT LEAVE UNTIL I FELT SAFE. SATURDAY I READ IN THE PAPER THAT A WOMAN JUMPED OFF THE BRIDGE AT THE EXACT MOMENT I SEEN THAT CAR PARKED ON THE SIDE OF THE ROAD.THE PAPER SAID SHE PICKED UP THE HELPLINE PHONE BUT DIDNT TALK TO ANYONE, THAT SHE WAS ADAMANT ABOUT DYING; THEY ULTIMATELY FOUND HER BODY FRIDAY MORNING. ONCE I SEEN THAT I FROZE, IT ALL STARTED TO MAKE SENCE AND I FELT LIKE SOMETHING WAS WRONG BECAUSE SOMETHING WAS IN FACT WRONG. I WAS COMPELLED TO LOOK FOR SOMEONE BECAUSE THERE WAS SOMEONE TO LOOK FOR. I GUESS I WAS TOO LATE BUT I CANT HELP BUT TO THINK IF I DIDNT STOP FOR A RED LIGHT OR IF I WAS GOING A LITTLE BIT FASTER I COULD OF STOPPED HER.I KNOW WHAT ITS LIKE TO BE IN THE STATE OF MIND OF DEATH,TO BE IN SO MUCH PAIN THAT NOTHNG ELSE MATTERS ANYMORE AND ALL YOU CAN DO IS END THE PAIN THE ONLY WAY YOU KNOW HOW.BEING WHERE I AM TODAY, IM NOT INVISIBLE TO PAIN BUT NOW I HAVE ONE TOOL THAT PROTECTS ME FROM GIVING UP,HOPE. NOT SAYNG THAT THS WOMAN HAD NO HOPE, SHE JUST COULDN'T SEE IT.IF ONLY I COULD HAVE GOTTEN TO HER AND PRAYED WITH HER OR HELD HER HAND OR JUST SIMPLY GIVEN HER A HUG I COULD HAVE SAVED A LIFE AND A SOUL. SOMETIMES, JUST A HUG CAN SAVE SOMEONES LIFE. I KNOW WHAT ITS LIKE TO HURT. WITH CHRIST I CANT SEE ANY REASON IN HELL WORTH TAKNG MY OWN LIFE; IVE BEN BEATEN, RAPED, STABBED, HOMELESS, WATCHED MY CAR GET REPOSSESSED, HAVE A GUN HELD TO MY HEAD, KICKED IN THE FACE, PREGNANT AND ALONE, STRUNG OUT, ALL OF IT, SO THERES NOTHNG ANYONE CAN TELL ME THAT COULD JUSTIFY

SUICIDE..NO MATTER HOW DARK IT LOOKS, HOW FOGGY THE ROAD LOOKS, HOW MUCH IT HURTS, HOW HOPELESS IT SEEMS, HOW ASHAMED YOU FEEL OR HOW UNBEARABLE IT IS. IM SORROWFUL OVER THAT WOMAN BECAUSE SHE DIDN'T HAVE TO DIE SO SOON.WHATEVER WAS GOING ON IN HER LIFE WASN'T WORTH THE END.I PRAISE GOD FOR ALLOWING ME TO HEAR HIM THAT DAY BECAUSE EVEN THOUGH I DIDN'T GET TO THAT WOMAN IN TIME I STILL CARED ABOUT HER AND PRAYED FOR HER SOUL AND THAT WAS ENOUGH TO GET THE DEVIL MAD...I REALIZED THAT THE ENEMY ATTACKED ME THE NEXT DAY FOR SIMPLY ATTEMPTING TO RUIN HIS PLAN..BUT I CANT FEAR SOMETHING IM MUCH MORE STRONGER THAN...IM NOT PERFECT BUT I DO HAVE SOMETHING I NEVER HAD BEFORE AND THAT IS HOPE! EVERYDAY IM STRIVING TO BE A BETTER CHILD OF GOD AND EVERYDAY I SEE HIS MERCY ON ME...EVEN IF THS IS THE LAST WORDS I SAY TO THS WORLD ILL STILL REJOICE BECAUSE I WAS ABLE TO PRAISE MY LORD.
~April 14, 2011

I added this entry into this book not show that God has let me go or that I have lost my faith, but to show how the demon of suicide affects even those who we aren't closely attached to and how that death affects even those who don't even know us.

This section is to show how the daily battles we face can dictate our world and our view points. I didn't know the woman in the story or what she was going through; but I have been where she was. I have spent many nights crying out to my Lord in agony because the trials of the day have beat me down so badly that I couldn't even breath. The woes of the week held me tightly by the throat and wouldn't let me speak. I felt that every light post I passed on the highway was erected for my demise, that every oncoming tractor trailer was where I needed to park my front bumper. It's a war that wages on inside your heart. The voices of your mistakes, the reflections of your words; it's a daily battle of give and not being able to take. The wonders of depression are defined by the world as being symptoms of a much larger illness; but here is where the spiritual aspect comes into play.

Ephesians 6:12

New Living Translation (NLT)

[12] For we are not fighting against flesh-and-blood enemies, but against evil rulers and authorities of the unseen world, against mighty powers in this dark world, and against evil spirits in the heavenly places.

For me, going to work and getting an attitude from my boss or being cut off in traffic would be the triggers to a night full of tears. The added stressor on an already fragile mind frame; but the word tells us that we are not wrestling with the flesh and blood. So the person in the grocery line who made a snarky comment about us underneath their breath is not the issue but the spirit that dwells within them is. Okay well easier said than done when you are already riddled with depressive and dark manifestations. While writing this section, I endured a devastating breakup. I gave my heart to this man for the first time in eight years. I vowed to myself that no man would get my heart without a down payment first and that was at 23 years of age. At 31, I found myself head first in the deep end of loss, emptiness, and questions that would never be answered. I gave my all to this man; everything but my body. I did everything right; seemingly. He had me on a string; so bad that I refused to see the other woman he entertained and the lack of concern he had for sticking to the promises he made to my children and I. this man poked and prodded to get into my closet and then used my skeletons to gang fight me in the middle of the street. He diagnosed me with an unrighteous intent and labeled me with his harsh words and assumptions. He left me at my lowest point and it devastated me. I was left with all this love and these broken promises of a future that he had no intention of giving. He broke my heart and my spirit. Daily I woke up and fought my reality searching for a way to rationalize the pain and gaping hole in my chest. Daily I fought the woman I used to be with the thoughts of the woman I was turned into. He left a shell of myself and every word I was delivered from since I got saved, was reattached to me with just one Facebook message. My daily battle was with the mirror and a soul that didn't want to die. I looked into my own eyes and I saw a woman who got whipped and chained but still put her armor back on before leaving the house. A woman who trusted a man with the safety of her heart and was still able to stand back up and let the right one in. I saw the pain in my triumph. I, for the first time in 31 years, saw who Marisa McClinton was. I discovered more about myself in that instant than I ever have in the past 30 years. I realized that the moment this so called "love of my life" didn't care was the instant that he put an extra "S" in my name like my absent father did when he came around every four years. Imagine how one letter of the alphabet could bring so much devastation. There I was broken and hurt all over again, and only because this man was assigned to my path to help catapult the pain needed to complete this book. I remember there was one day when I was praying in my car during my lunch break and I remembered this scripture and I began to look around and even in the mirror. I began to look at my circumstances and my depressive state in a new light. I began to look at what the devil was trying to do against me instead of what the world was trying to do to keep me bound. I realized that this is where I needed to stop handling a spiritual problem with a natural mind set. I had to approach the spirit with its own defenses and approach the world with its own. Daily I had to remind myself that the battle I was fighting in or at least laying in was a battle of the good and the evil after my own destiny. God made a promise to me on my head at conception and the devil made a counter offer once he saw the vision and outcome to that promise. It has been a battle that has been raging since I was born. But a battle that is not understood until we are born again. Now let me not confuse anyone here, it was not an easy endeavor; the concept of principalities is not an easy thing to remember when you are going through the fire and the rain, the hurt and the pain, and the fear and the jeers. I spent weeks of crying and cursing myself before I would remember that the battle does not belong to me. I am human and in my human mind I would fall before I got up. I would lay in the mud for days before the Lord would remind me of the grace and the love that he has for those who diligently seek him. It would take me having a complete nervous breakdown before I realized that God was by my side the entire time. That I am protected and that I am hidden from the rain. I can picture myself hiding behind the king of kings holding onto his arm tight like a small child holds onto a parent's leg when they encounter someone new in their presence. I would feel safe while I heard the bombs of life going off all around us. I would feel proud that my father wouldn't flinch or bender. I would feel hopeful because I could hear the shrieks of the enemies defeat; and then the fire would get to close to my side of the Lord. I would feel a scratch or a twinge of pain from the battle and I would begin to hyperventilate even in the Lords presence. I would begin to panic even while holding onto him with all of my might. "How could this be?" I asked myself. How could I be terrified while standing in the presence of the Lord? I was so backwards in my head and but so desperate in my heart. Daily I struggled with a different inconsistency. I struggled with a different version of the truth until I realized and learned that the truth only comes in one package. See this is the paradigm of being saved, sanctified, and filled with the holy ghost while fighting the fight of depression and suicide; The demons of the destructive layer of the pits of hell. The fact that the enemy is full aware of this weakness shows that the battle must be contained within the spiritual realm. While the world states that depression can be cured with medication and modern techniques; the heart and the pains within can only be addressed and healed by the one who created it. I have been on both sides of this; I have been on medication and I have been on the pills of prayer and while medication is essential for some forms of disease, the spiritual symptoms that depression and suicide carry must be adhered to as well. As a woman who is currently seeking the Lord for her wholeness, I know the lure of wanting an antidepressant to numb the pain of the past; but I have found the value and the victory in having the Lord deliver me of what it is I struggle with. A lot of times, I would be forced to push down emotions in order to make it through the day leaving me a walking time bomb of emotions. I stuffed myself like a thanksgiving turkey with my hatred, anger, and fear. I was packed to the brim with it by the time it exploded to the point of me being mere minutes away from death after my last suicide attempt. Even as I write this, I stand in the process of being purged. To have to re-feel those emotions, revisit those experiences, rehear those peoples comments, relearn how to exist without pain. Like I said previously about the regurgitation process; it doesn't feel good at all coming back up. I had to make a choice and I had to make a decision as to where I wanted to carry this battle and how I wanted to define my "daily". Yes my "daily" may still carry some small form of pain and confusion but I now am more aware of what the battle entails and who the general was leading the army. Ask yourself, how do you define your daily battle?

Job 7:1-8

New Living Translation (NLT)

7 "Is not all human life a struggle?

Our lives are like that of a hired hand,

[2] like a worker who longs for the shade,

like a servant waiting to be paid.

[3] I, too, have been assigned months of futility,

long and weary nights of misery.

[4] Lying in bed, I think, 'When will it be morning?'

But the night drags on, and I toss till dawn.

[5] My body is covered with maggots and scabs.

My skin breaks open, oozing with pus.

[6] "My days fly faster than a weaver's shuttle.

They end without hope.

[7] O God, remember that my life is but a breath,

and I will never again feel happiness.

[8] You see me now, but not for long.

You will look for me, but I will be gone

1 Corinthians 10:12-13

New Living Translation (NLT)

[12] If you think you are standing strong, be careful not to fall. [13] The temptations in your life are no different from what others experience. And God is faithful. He will not allow the temptation to be more than you can stand. When you are tempted, he will show you a way out so that you can endure

CHAPTER FOUR
And yet the world says

Romans 12:2

New Living Translation (NLT)

[2] Don't copy the behavior and customs of this world, but let God transform you into a new person by changing the way you think. Then you will learn to know God's will for you, which is good and pleasing and perfect.

I have discovered over the years that there are many different types of depression defined by both the world and the Christian community. I first want to define depression from the worlds standpoint because the world is first to put a scientific and chemical makeup to the phenomena of depression.

According to Webster's dictionary, depression is defined as:

de pres sion

noun \di-ˈpre-shən, dē-\

: a state of feeling sad

: a serious medical condition in which a person feels very sad, hopeless, and unimportant and often is unable to live in a normal way

: a period of time in which there is little economic activity and many people do not have jobs

("Depression - Definition and More from the Free Merriam-Webster Dictionary", n.d., p. 1)

The medical world defines depression with several different sub categories that carry different symptoms and triggers; for instance, *WebMD* has seven different "types" of depression that carry extremely different symptoms for each. The seven include Postpartum, Psychotic, Bipolar or Manic, Atypical, Chronic, and Major depressive disorder. ("Types of Depression: Major, Chronic, Manic, and More Types", n.d., p. 1) each of these different types are common amongst many people within our society. Despite the amount and variety of types, depression is still looked upon as something that mirrors a defect or a broken piece of the human psyche. Some of these symptoms may occur on a regular basis or may come and go based on circumstances and/or seasons. Postpartum depression can occur in women who have just given birth or even about to give birth which is called pre-partum depression. Both of these types of depression are commonly linked to the hormonal changes that a woman faces during and after pregnancy and child birthing. While depression may not be diagnosed as such, the symptoms may be evident for an extended period of time before any diagnosis is considered. For example, "One in five pregnant women may be experiencing symptoms of depression, but few are getting help for it, a new University of Michigan study finds." ("Pre-partum depression | Hormonal Pregnant Woman", n.d., p. 1) One in five pregnant women seems a bit excessive but it shows that depression symptoms are more common than expected and the lack of treatment is just as common. One can only speculate as to why the treatment numbers are so low, but the stigma that being diagnosed as "depressed" is a major human flaw, doesn't help push the importance of finding the right kind of help. When I was 16 years old, I was diagnosed as Bipolar or having a "chemical imbalance". I was told that I have rash swings of my mod from extreme highs of happiness and energy and then extreme dips into sadness and despair. I was put on two medications that suppressed and numbed my ability to feel anything. I was a walking zombie who floated in between somber and completely brain dead. I wasn't sure of my surroundings and what used to make me happy no longer had any effect on me. What used to bring me joy, no longer made any sense to me and actually made me kind of confused. I hated the way I felt, so I took myself off the medication; which I do not condone or suggest for anyone, this is just what my experience was. I do commend the medical community for making antidepressants more flexible in the way they affect a persons' response time and emotional control; but I have always made the recommendation to have a person seek the help that is best for them and to not solely rely on the results of his/ her neighbor. The difficult part about these medications is that the pharmaceutical community is making a mighty profit off of the medications prescribed to the thousands of newly diagnosed depressive disorders; making the medication route questionable and sketchy at best. I have seen the long term results of anti-depressive medications and I, personally, feel that a person should receive many forms of professional and spiritual opinions on their diagnosis before settling in for life on one diagnosis. Depression in the medical field comes with many different triggers; for example, seasonal depressions or SAD is known to be triggered by hormonal signals in the brain that are automatically triggered at specified times of the year. Some know this type of depression as being associated with cabin fever or winter blues, but in rare forms can occur in the spring and summer months. Scientists are leaning towards the excessive and/ or stunted production of serotonin which is a neurotransmitter that has a soothing and calming effect on the individual. The fluctuations of this neurotransmitter is said to be associated with the lack of sunlight during the winter months and the excessive amount of light during the summer months. SAD sufferers tend to vary in their symptoms and their ability to naturally overcome the symptoms they do experience. ("Types of Depression: Major, Chronic, Manic, and More Types", n.d., p. 1)

While science has turned the depressive state into a complex novel of medical terms, symptoms, and triggers, there is an entirely different side to this state of thinking, feeling, and acting. There is a spiritual side to the scientific diagnosis of the world that not only does the Bible address but the Christian community has also studied and formed a diagnosis of its own. From the Christian standpoint there are eight different types of depression; situational, clinical, chronic, external, personal, mental, spiritual, and physical. Each of these types carry a specified trigger both naturally and spiritually along with a word to coincide the spiritual occurrence of that state.

Situation depression is, as the name implies, brought on by adverse situations. Generally, the depression clears with time, as the situation is resolved or accepted. Situational depression isn't necessarily bad. Often, it's a reasonable and appropriate response to the pain of a fallen world.

Lamentations 3:1-18

New Living Translation (NLT)

3 I am the one who has seen the afflictions

that come from the rod of the Lord's anger.

[2] He has led me into darkness,

shutting out all light.

[3] He has turned his hand against me

again and again, all day long.

[4] He has made my skin and flesh grow old.

He has broken my bones.

[5] He has besieged and surrounded me

with anguish and distress.

[6] He has buried me in a dark place,

like those long dead.

[7] He has walled me in, and I cannot escape.

He has bound me in heavy chains.

[8] And though I cry and shout,

he has shut out my prayers.

[9] He has blocked my way with a high stone wall;

he has made my road crooked.

[10] He has hidden like a bear or a lion,

waiting to attack me.

[11] He has dragged me off the path and torn me in pieces,

leaving me helpless and devastated.

[12] He has drawn his bow

and made me the target for his arrows.

[13] He shot his arrows

deep into my heart.

[14] My own people laugh at me.

All day long they sing their mocking songs.

[15] He has filled me with bitterness

and given me a bitter cup of sorrow to drink.

[16] He has made me chew on gravel.

He has rolled me in the dust.

[17] Peace has been stripped away,

and I have forgotten what prosperity is.

[18] I cry out, "My splendor is gone!

Everything I had hoped for from the Lord is lost!"

Clinical depression is an ongoing condition that lasts every day for most of the day and for longer than two weeks. Clinical depression interferes with day-to-day life at work, school, and home. Sleep habits are also disturbed. Clinical depression can be triggered by trauma, but it is not caused by medication or a medical condition.

Chronic depression is less intense than clinical depression, but can last much longer—two years at least. It's characterized by fatigue, sadness, and general malaise, and it can be punctuated by bouts of clinical depression. Chronic depression doesn't feel good, but it doesn't typically affect lifestyle or the ability to work.

Before the fall of man, there was no sin, no shame, no fear, and no depression. Depression is a result of the fall, and those who suffer from depression find that it has ramifications in all parts of human life—external, personal, mental, physical, and spiritual.

External Depression has a strong genetic component; however, many depressive episodes are triggered by an external situation. The death of a loved one is a common trigger. Sustained stress, wintertime, and even a busy life can also lead to depression.

Psalm 143:3-4

New Living Translation (NLT)

[3] My enemy has chased me.

He has knocked me to the ground

and forces me to live in darkness like those in the grave.

[4] I am losing all hope;

I am paralyzed with fear.

Personal choices play a role in depression. It's been said that depression is sin, but it's more accurate to say that sin leads to and feeds depression. Depression can be caused by alcohol and drug abuse, indulging in anger and self-centeredness, and other self-destructive behaviors. Sin always has negative consequences, and part of any therapy for depression should include an analysis of what sins could be exacerbating the situation.

Psalm 32:3-5

New Living Translation (NLT)

[3] When I refused to confess my sin,

my body wasted away,

and I groaned all day long.

[4] Day and night your hand of discipline was heavy on me.

My strength evaporated like water in the summer heat. Interlude

[5] Finally, I confessed all my sins to you

and stopped trying to hide my guilt.

I said to myself, "I will confess my rebellion to the Lord."

And you forgave me! All my guilt is gone.

Mental Depression is driven by negative feelings, perceptions, and thoughts. Unbiblical beliefs about one's value and ability often contribute to depression. The Bible exhorts us to take thoughts captive to concentrate on the truth of a situation and not a faulty perception and to rely on God's Word and not our feelings or what a person thinks, feels, and chooses to believe, true or not, can have physical repercussions. Refusing to believe the power and love of God and concentrating on brokenness and pain would make anyone depressed.

2 Corinthians 10:5

New Living Translation (NLT)

[5] We destroy every proud obstacle that keeps people from knowing God. We capture their rebellious thoughts and teach them to obey Christ.

John 8:32

New Living Translation (NLT)

[32] And you will know the truth, and the truth will set you free.

Spiritual depression has a definite spiritual element. It can be one of Satan's tools to take Christians out of the work of the Kingdom. Depression can affect our view of God and sap our joy. It is impossible to live a Spirit-guided life without joy. Sometimes, depression may be caused by direct demonic activity but not always. How we handle depression is a highly spiritual matter. The Bible says to cast all our cares on God, A remedy for a "downcast soul" is to place one's trust in the God who saves. "Why are you cast down, O my soul, and why are you in turmoil within me? Hope in God; for I shall again praise him, my salvation and my God"

Psalm 42:11

New Living Translation (NLT)

[11] Why am I discouraged?

Why is my heart so sad?

I will put my hope in God!

I will praise him again—

my Savior and my God!

Galatians 5:22

New Living Translation (NLT)

[22] But the Holy Spirit produces this kind of fruit in our lives: love, joy, peace, patience, kindness, goodness, faithfulness,

Philippians 4:4

New Living Translation (NLT)

[4] Always be full of joy in the Lord. I say it again—rejoice!

1 Samuel 16:14

New Living Translation (NLT)

- [14] Now the Spirit of the Lord had left Saul, and the Lord sent a tormenting spirit[a] that filled him with depression and fear

1 Peter 5:7

New Living Translation (NLT)

- [7] Give all your worries and cares to God, for he cares about you.

Physical depression can affect our physical bodies in several ways. An injury or illness can trigger depression and then hinder rehabilitation, causing a vicious cycle. Insomnia can do the same. Depression can also be caused by a simple brain chemical or hormonal imbalance that is easily solved with medication. Treatment may require an attack on several fronts—temporary medication to relax the body and relieve the mind, adjustments to the diet, confession of sin, and spiritual counsel. Sometimes, the victim of depression can just ride it out, trusting that God will bring comfort and that the situation will change. Other times, counseling and medication are required. God desires His children to know joy. Bouts of depression can serve to bring us closer to Him through our struggles, "My flesh and my heart may fail, but God is the strength of my heart and my portion forever"

Romans 5:3-5

New Living Translation (NLT)

[3] We can rejoice, too, when we run into problems and trials, for we know that they help us develop endurance. [4] And endurance develops strength of character, and character strengthens our confident hope of salvation. [5] And this hope will not lead to disappointment. For we know how dearly God loves us, because he has given us the Holy Spirit to fill our hearts with his love.

1 Peter 1:6-7

New Living Translation (NLT)

[6] So be truly glad. There is wonderful joy ahead, even though you have to endure many trials for a little while. [7] These trials will show that your faith is genuine. It is being tested as fire tests and purifies gold—though your faith is far more precious than mere gold. So when your faith remains strong through many trials, it will bring you much praise and glory and honor on the day when Jesus Christ is revealed to the whole world.

Psalm 73:26

New Living Translation (NLT)

[26] My health may fail, and my spirit may grow weak,

but God remains the strength of my heart;

he is mine forever.

("How should a Christian deal with depression? What does the Bible say about depression?" 2011, p. 1-2)

Depression is something that people from all walks of life and faith bases can experience. Nothing about depression is sinful to Christ and depression is not necessarily brought on by sin, but when it is experienced, the sufferer should know that Christ is on their side and that the first step is discovering the cause and the root so to lead to treatment and healing. The world has allowed the misunderstanding of this occurrence to cause the onset to become something of shame. I have seen many churches view depression as something that needs to be swept underneath the rug and many worldly associations treat depression as a form of leprosy. For a person who suffers from depression and the fear of ridicule, confession can be something that is terrifying and crippling to the persons healing process. I have experienced many times over that sometimes reaching out for help can be more painful than going through it alone. Experiencing depression alone can be a dark and lonely process; but going through the process with a world that doesn't understand can be confusing and painful. From the spiritual aspect, understanding the signs and symptoms of the depressed state is essential to beginning the process of moving forward toward wholeness and wellness in Christ. Along with the world, the first step includes confession and acceptance of what is being experienced.

There are many statistics that paint many different pictures of what depression is and how it is being treating. According to the American Association of suicidology only about 25% of those diagnosed with depression are receiving the proper treatment. Once treatment is adequately given about 60 – 80% of it is extremely effective. (AAS, 2009, p. 1-4) commonly, if depression is left untreated, the symptoms can drive the sufferer to more complex disorders such as suicide, alcohol, and substance abuse.

To share some more essential statistics about the common link between depression and suicide:

- Major depression is the psychiatric diagnosis most commonly associated with suicide. Lifetime risk of suicide among patients with untreated depressive disorder is nearly 20% (Gotlib & Hammen, 2002). The suicide risk among treated patients is 141/100,000 (Isacsson et al, 2000).
- About 2/3 of people who complete suicide are depressed at the time of their deaths.
- About 7 out of every hundred men and 1 out of every hundred women who have been diagnosed with depression in their lifetime will go on to complete suicide.
- The risk of suicide in people with major depression is about 20 times that of the general population.
- Individuals who have had multiple episodes of depression are at greater risk for suicide than those who have had one episode.
- People who have a dependence on alcohol or drugs in addition to being depressed are at greater risk for suicide (AAS, 2009, p. 1-4)

The Battled Christian

One of the greatest things we can do as a church and as a society is to understand the complexities of the occurrence of depression and how it leads to suicide. I have heard the remarks concerning people who do successfully attempt suicide and they have been less than favorable. I agree that suicide is hurtful for those the victim has left behind, but I feel that as a society, suicide is preventable and there are many ways that we can assist those who suffer from depression and hopelessness. I have experienced many times the loneliness of being judged for my feelings. There is a sense of misunderstanding the presence of depression and in turn causes for a judgmental attacking of the victims' emotions and feelings.

I suffered from depression for a great portion of my life. There have been people that I have confessed to about my depression that have been supportive and helpful with my recovery; and I have encountered people who have judged me, criticized me, and bad mouthed me out of pure lack of knowledge and compassion for what I am enduring. I have had people treat me like I was a broken toy and handle me roughly which ultimately made my condition worse on a daily basis. A lot of the efforts of me being able to heal and move forward from my symptoms have been thwarted by the negativity and lack of support of those surrounding me. It's difficult when you want to heal and be whole, but his world looks at you and handles you based on your symptoms and not who you are. While depression is an occurrence and a tool for the enemies' advancement, I do not believe that is a persons' characteristic or a persons' genetic makeup. The gravest mistake that a society can make is to label those who suffer from depression as being "difficult", " complicated" "toxic"; these labels only slow the healing process and take away from the persons God given personality and purpose. God has not instructed us to judge someone based on his or her mood, but to treat others with love and compassion; and in my experiences, this type of treatment could mean the difference between life and death for someone who has lost all hope.

CHAPTER FIVE
When enough is enough

Matthew 6:33

New Living Translation (NLT)

[33] Seek the Kingdom of God above all else, and live righteously, and he will give you everything you need.

Psalm 30:11

New Living Translation (NLT)

[11] You have turned my mourning into joyful dancing.

You have taken away my clothes of mourning and clothed me with joy

Romans 8:38-39

New Living Translation (NLT)

[38] And I am convinced that nothing can ever separate us from God's love. Neither death nor life, neither angels nor demons, [neither] our fears for today nor our worries about tomorrow — not even the powers of hell can separate us from God's love. [39] No power in the sky above or in the earth below — indeed, nothing in all creation will ever be able to separate us from the love of God that is revealed in Christ Jesus our Lord.

There comes a point where the pain a person feels is so consuming that the only thing that is left is to reach for help. I spent that past week wrestling with the pain, rejection, fear, and complete mistrust of my past. I was faced with my final attempt on my life. I grew anxious and terrified of what was next for me. I couldn't see myself for the purpose I was born to fulfill. I couldn't see my children and the pain they would suffer at the hand of my disappearance; I couldn't see the tears of the world from a book that wasn't completed because the author couldn't stand long enough to be saved. I couldn't see any of that until I found myself on my kitchen floor with a knife in my hand. I woke up out of an anxiety attack and saw the pan I was about to cause. I awoke to the realization that the only thing that I was doing was running from my issues; running from the prayers begging God to show me myself and take my pain out by the root. I forgot that when God takes things out, he has to usually pass them back through the way they got in; the heart. Like the food we ingest daily, when something doesn't agree with us, the human body will eject it by passing it back through the way it entered; the mouth. The pain I carried on my shoulders for so many years we buried deep within the soil of my gut. I ingested it and buried it so deep within me that the only safe way to get it back out was to eject it back the way it came in. just like that ejecting food, the process of regurgitation is painful and distasteful. It hurts the throat and it burns the stomach. The process of regurgitating the past burns the belly of the soul and rips the throat of the spirit right into pieces. The outcome is the miracle of healing but the process is the wretchedness of shaping and molding. I have always ran from this process; in my spirit I would push myself to complete this race and I was determined to come out the victor; but in my heart and in my mind the fire would get too hot and I would run with my tail between my legs. It's not easy, but then God didn't promise that any of this life would be easy. I got tired and fed up with myself. I had enough of the rollercoaster emotions and the desire to end my life but the will to live. The battle deep within myself between the hurt and pain of my past and the ordained future of my manifest destiny. I struggled with pain of abuse and rape, I struggled with rejection and fear but I heard the voice of God tell me that I was to preach to the nations, that I was to teach to the children, and I was to carry forth words of healing and life; and here I am fighting the demon of death daily. I had enough of the inconsistency, I had enough of the confusion, and enough of the anger towards myself for not knowing. I had enough of the issues I was dealing with, the problems that would arise and the frustration my past would cause me even today. I had enough of the life that I created for myself. Enough of the pain, the hurt, the sadness and depression. I had enough of feeling defeated while the world passed me by. I got tired of being the tail and wanted to the head. I was sick of my old self, but wasn't able to let her go. I knew in my mind that I had to turn down the old wo-man and put on the new creature that God has rebirthed; but when I looked at myself, all I saw was the girl who the worlds burden and the worlds scape goat. I was beyond low esteem and beyond low self-confidence; I couldn't face myself at all. I could walk in the victory that the Lord said I had on my head. I wasn't able to face the greatness that God placed within me. I was blinded by my own mistakes and shortcomings. I was afraid of being happy and afraid of the good side of life. I was terrified of disappointment which made me afraid to stretch out towards the excellence that I was promised. I feared life and all it had to offer. But then something happened that made me get tired of being tired. Something clicked in my brain that made me realize that continuing on this road would only lead to a disgraceful death; which is what I didn't want. I looked at my behavior and my words and my thoughts from the past few years and I saw how ugly it all was. I saw how retched and nasty it was and looked up and saw how it mourned the Holy Spirit greatly; I was stuck, I was trapped in the age I was when I first faced my underwhelming self. Almost like an addict is said to remain in the mental capacity of when they first began the addiction for as long as they are on that substance. I had a boyfriend who was in recovery when we reignited a very old flame and I would see that some of his behaviors mimicked that of the young boy that I knew many, many years ago. It was only after speaking to his sponsor that many times an alcoholic or addict will remain in the mental and emotional age of when they began their addiction until the addiction and the causes of such are addressed in the proper way. I often looked back at this bit of information and saw a lot of that theory in myself; but the only difference is that I am not addicted to a substance, but to my pain. At the age of 26 I realized that I was addicted to my pain. I spent so many years in pain and in sorrow that I've grown to become comfortable with it; like a sack of grief and misery engulfed me for comfort and warmth like a caterpillar with its cocoon. I was afraid of letting go because it meant that I had to place myself out of the darkness and into the light where people who hurt, lie, and steal could see me, making me vulnerable and at their mercy. I felt like if I didn't expect the pain or disappointment to come then I would be hurt 100 times when it did come. But I had to ask myself, "How can I even guarantee that pain is to come?" how am I so certain that joy, happiness, and peace isn't in my destiny? Questions that were logical but yet had no logical answers. I feared what "could" happen more than I appreciated what "was" happening. I spent more time looking for the punch line than I did enjoying the story. Like a car accident, bracing for impact. I remember when I was 17 years old and I was hit head on by a drunk driver. I seen the truck coming and I knew he was going to hit me and all I could do was just brace for the impact. I tried to compensate the hit in my mind, but no matter how much I curled into a ball, the impact still felt like I was exploding from the inside out. There is no bracing for the impact of life. There is no amount of preparation to prepare a person for the impact of being betrayed, lied to, beat up, talked about, left behind, or any other horrible aspect of human existence. The fact remained that yes, I was a girl whom experienced a large amount of hurt and yes I was a woman who held onto every single thread of those hurts and carried them like a wallet full of cash. My eyes opened to that fact and I was able to see myself carrying around these endless threads of hurt and fear. I saw how hunched over I was, how tired I was, how low I was. I saw myself in utter despair and all it did was make me feel even more depressed until I was ready to say "no more". I got tired of seeing myself like that. I got tired of seeing my pain on my face. I got tired of feeling my burdens in my bones. I got tired of feeling all the negative words of my past in my veins. I got sick of it and I was ready to move on and move forward. I was ready to leave that heavy and sickened woman behind and step into this dynamic existence of grace and valor. It took work, work that I was finally ready to continue. It took a fire that burned deep within me that was ready to burn into the night and outlast the storms. I had to be ready, I had to see myself as more and trust God for my "more". I had to get back up, I had to look at myself as more than a burden to myself and this world but as a woman with ability and a destination. I had to force my face out of the mud and force my feet to get moving. It hurt, my bones were weak and my mind was cluttered. My nerves were shot and my eyes were cried out. I couldn't feel the air in my lungs anymore. The peace I knew on a part time basis was long gone and the hope I once knew was invisible; but I had to rise. I had to stand on those fragile bones and push with those weak lungs. I had to continue and to find purpose in my hopelessness. I had to find the will to stand because the longer I spent down in the mud, the closer death got. I took my complete emotional exhaustion to catapult me into the will and want to get up and fight.

Psalm 23:4

"4 even when I walk

through the darkest valley,

I will not be afraid,

for you are close beside me.

Your rod and your staff

protect and comfort me"

This scripture rang with me during my darkest hour and then I realized that it took trust; trust to know that God is yet with me in the midst of my darkest hour and my deepest valley. Trust that his rod and staff will comfort me in the perfect time and perfect will. It took fight and it took dedication to get me to this point.

This was a point in my life where I had to put into practice everything that I have learned and prayed for my entire saved life. I had to trust God to get me on my feet. I had to believe him to comfort me and draw me near to him even though I was walking through a valley of evil and death. I had to fix my eyes on the Lord and have him show me how to get up and move forward even when my feet ached with sorrow and hindrances. I had to look to the hills from which my help cometh and fix my heart on the process of healing and purging. I had to view myself through Gods eyes. I had to see what the kingdom saw for me and not what the world said to me. I had to remove the dead skin of the past and put on the lotion of the magnificence of the future at the Lords right hand. Enough was enough for me when I realized that every hurt and offense I had ever encountered was dictating my day, my minutes, my hours, and my mouth. Every disrespect and every embarrassment was pulling me and pushing me with every breath. I was a slave to my pain and a hostage to my experiences. Enough was enough and I had to evolve and run towards the woman of valor that the Lord called me to be. I desired and yearned to put on the new woman, the new creature, the new mind frame. I looked in the mirror and saw on my face the lines of the pain I endured, the wrinkles of the tears I've cried, and the frown of the rejection I have faced. Enough is enough when you look at yourself and see more for your future than your declining health, when you can picture yourself walking taller and speaking louder. When you can see the smile on your face and the joy beaming from your heart. You know enough is enough when you put down the bottle of pills and you tell the devil 'no'. There comes a point when a woman must remind herself that her life is setup for a victory. That the line in the sand comes when she is tired of crying and tired of fighting death. Enough is enough when the voice that once cracked is now strong enough to tell the story. Enough is enough for me when I am able to sit here and release these emotions for the world to see. Yes, lord I have reached my "enough is enough" moment.

Psalm 40:2

New Living Translation (NLT)

[2] He lifted me out of the pit of despair,

out of the mud and the mire.

He set my feet on solid ground

and steadied me as I walked along.

CHAPTER SIX
There's no "I" in recovery

Psalm 40:9-10

New Living Translation (NLT)

[9] I have told all your people about your justice.

I have not been afraid to speak out,

as you, O Lord, well know.

[10] I have not kept the good news of your justice hidden in my heart;

I have talked about your faithfulness and saving power.

I have told everyone in the great assembly

of your unfailing love and faithfulness.

My journey as a Christian woman who suffered from depression most of her life and suicidal thoughts and actions, has not come to a complete end; because this journey towards discovery and healing is a lifelong endeavor. On a daily basis I see myself as many things, from a mother, a student, a care giver, a worshiper, an intercessor, a victim, a survivor, a lover, a fighter, a people pleaser, a friend, a sister, a child, a conqueror, an author, a columnist, and a woman with a purpose. I see many things when I look in my own eyes, but the one thing I don't see is the pain I've endured. Although I have felt the bottom of the swamp of hurt and disappointment, by the grace of God I have no succumbed to the mercy of self-pity.

Romans 8:18-21

New Living Translation (NLT)

[18] Yet what we suffer now is nothing compared to the glory he will reveal to us later. [19] For all creation is waiting eagerly for that future day when God will reveal who his children really are. [20] Against its will, all creation was subjected to God's curse. But with eager hope, [21] the creation looks forward to the day when it will join God's children in glorious freedom from death and decay

John 16:33

New Living Translation (NLT)

[33] I have told you all this so that you may have peace in me. Here on earth you will have many trials and sorrows. But take heart, because I have overcome the world."

The Battled Christian

As being a Christian, we are taught that we should look towards the Lord for all of our needs and to be not influenced by this world but to be changed and molded by the love and example of Christ. I have adopted this concept and have strived to live this very practice on a daily basis; but as a woman who suffers from depression in a world of judgments and criticisms, I am in a battle with myself and my spirit. For the past 10 years I have self-medicated with men, drugs, alcohol, suppression, writing, and anything else that prevented me from feeling what I was experiencing. I bottled up my emotions and suppressed them to the point of utter confusion and loss of who I was and my character. I wanted "appear" as normal as possible to people around me. The pain was so great that being able to get up and function each day would not have happened unless I had a drug in my system or a bottle in my hand. Once I grew out of the chemical dependency, I turned to men and sexual experience to distract me from what I was feeling and what I was trying to hide. I used sex to keep men from learning about the real me and the real battle I was facing each day. The result was temporary because once the man left, I was faced with myself; the only difference was that I was in the dark and now I had two children to show for it. There was no healing in the methods I used; just distraction and suppression. None of the attempts to release my pain worked towards actual release, but ran fast towards the detachedness of my true self and what I have walked through. I didn't allow myself to feel, I didn't allow myself to experience; out of embarrassment, I didn't allow myself to rationalize and conclude about what I have been through. I skipped over it and thought I was doing the right thing by not paying attention to the tears that fell in the middle of the night once another one night stand left the bed. I was self-medicating life and numbing the effects of living just so I could experience a false sense of existence for a mere 24 hour period. Nothing I did was appropriate and nothing I believed was actually happening. I was jaded and dazed. I was lying to myself about what life actually was. I didn't want to feel and I didn't want to know. I didn't want to be sure of the pain I endured, I only wanted to forget who I was and hope that I would wake up a new creature. For as long as I was walking in my own stew, I would never reach that perfect, self-euphoria that I dreamed up in my head for 26 years. I had to wake up and I had to stop moving for a moment. I had to seek help that was outside of myself. I had to do something different this time. Writing this book helped me to "feel". After my last break up, I felt lost and empty. I felt like my own future was cold and desolate. Despite my spirit, my flesh wanted to lay down and die; but there was a new flame in my heart. Something new burned inside of me and it was unfamiliar. I knew this time I had to "feel" my way through. I had to choose not to suppress and crawl forward, but to actually feel my way in the dark and stand and WALK forward. Normally I would run because it would hurt so badly; I self-medicated because it felt so rotten. I felt sick in my body and my bones felt like coals. I've endured the worst parts of human existence and each time I suppressed the pain because the sense of doom was simply unbearable. This time was different; I looked my pain in the eye; I confronted it. I was determined to heal and determined to make it through this and not just past it. I couldn't go over it, under it, below it, or around it; I had to go through it. The days moved so slowly; the pain burned so bad. I was battered and my wounds festered with infection and infliction. I felt it for once and it was raw. The burning pulsed through my veins like an air bubble headed straight towards my heart. The embarrassment of a love lost banged against my skull like a pendulum of spikes. I curled from the knife in my gut plunged from the depths of my loneliness. I fell into a pit of lions who fed on my fear and chewed on my failure; but my soul wouldn't die so I had to keep pushing. It became unbearable some days so I would try to run back to what I was familiar with; but nothing worked. This time my purpose wouldn't let my pain triumph. I begged and pleaded with God for something, anything to ease the pain and he just stood there. He watched me squirm and curl up from the fire and stood firm with only his right hand upon my back. I twisted in my own skin and flopped in my agony; but still my soul wouldn't die. It was my season to "feel" and man oh man was I feeling it. I got angry because I didn't understand why I was "feeling" and the man that caused this wasn't "feeling a thing. I was mad at myself because I let this happen; I let him in and now I am left a scorched piece of meat underneath the fridge after a kids birthday party. I couldn't imagine how this could ever turn out to be for the good of anything; but my soul wouldn't die. My dad told me that I "wasn't rejected, but protected". Seriously?! Protected from what? How or what could I have been protected from if I am already feeling this bad? I've been beat up and cheated on so what could this man possibly have done so much worse than what I have already endured? A crazy thought from an emotionally battered woman. I had no one; I saw no one. I was alone on this earth because nobody understood my pain and nobody understood my death. BUT GOD. My team consisted of my undying soul and my unfailing father. There was no "I" in my circumstances at all.

Psalm 43:4-5

New Living Translation (NLT)

[4] There I will go to the altar of God,

to God — the source of all my joy.

I will praise you with my harp,

O God, my God!

[5] Why am I discouraged?

Why is my heart so sad?

I will put my hope in God!

I will praise him again —

my Savior and my God!

The Battled Christian

It was one, cold night in March when I reached out to God. I grew up in the church and it was my foundation of the Lord that was deep within my heart and embedded in my mind. Out of all the suicide attempts, the mistakes, the cuss words, the drugs, the valleys, the anger, the pain, I was still a child of the living God. I was still a woman that was able to be saved, and I was still being protected and looked after by the one who created me. I had hope even when I threw it away. I couldn't see it, I couldn't hear it, and I couldn't understand it but I heard a voice that was so loud that none of my problems could reach me. Three months pregnant with my head in the toilet from morning sickness for the fourth hour in a row, I saw myself as more than anything I have ever been through in my previous years on the bottom. I was truly on the bottom of the barrel and this time with my head in the toilet. I sat on the floor and cried so hard that even the vomit had to cease. I wept inside the toilet and I yelled out to God in the devils face. I knew Gods name, but I couldn't of approached him with all of my shame. I felt hopeless and yet hopeful. I knew that there was a place inside of me that could have been saved; but I couldn't have done it alone. Alone I was defeated, mangled, and cast down; but with Christ I became strong, dynamic, joyous, and free. Over the six years that I have journeyed through salvation, I have found the love that I was searching for with all of those men, I found the respect that I couldn't find at the end of someone's fist, I found the comfort that I begged from all the drugs and alcohol; I found a place that allowed me to be me, whoever that was. Not every day was butterflies and unicorns; I've spent many nights pushing on the door that kept the pain of my past out of my face. I couldn't avoid it anymore, the elephant in the room. There came a point where some of those hurts came seeping out of me like a leaky faucet. Some of the smaller scale issues melted off of me like a piece of old skin in the hot summer sun; but some of the larger scale problems began to rip me to shreds on the inside like a weed Wacker in a field of dandelions. I was dreading the nightfall because that meant that I was going to have to feel. I was going to have to face my past, my hurts, my pains, my disappointments, my abuse, my rape, my fear, my anger, my embarrassment, my pride, my regret. It meant that I would have to discover the real me and actually I've with her. The worst moment of my life came when that door came flying open and I wasn't ready for the gust of bleeding memories that was assigned to my face. I could no longer run, and I could no longer hide. I was a woman who was about to go face first in the gully of my trauma; how retched.

But this time something was different, this time I was a different person in a different state. I was saved and I had the eyes of Christ on my forehead. I wasn't alone, I was prepared with a gift; I had the gift of the Holy Spirit. I was a woman who had an army behind her and to be honest, I was in the midst of the one who knew my pain and knew my experiences before I ever lived them. It felt different. Even in the presence of my greatest enemy, I, my journey and my works were different. As I began to feel, I learned to share and as I began to share, I learned the graciousness of using pain to conquer evil. My transparency ran the enemy off and brought me closer to my creator. My purpose was in my pain and my reason for living was embedded deep in the valleys of my heart. My hands shook with fear of judgment but then I was reminded that the only one who could judge me was already on my side. I was beginning to be free; free of bondage and free of imprisonment. Even now, not every day is perfect, I am still feeling and I am still experiencing those moments; but the difference now is that instead of covering up my pain, I have learned to embrace it and feel it through. I have learned to identify myself both through Christ and through the world; both with my depression and with my joy. I am a work in progress and my story is yet to be finished until the day I am called home; but I can stand firm in my iniquity and declare that I am nowhere near the girl I was at the beginning of this story.

The Battled Christian

An excerpt from my book "*The Suicidal Christian: the battle is the mind*": "*I am a Christian and I tried to kill myself. Not because God failed me or because my church failed me but because I was overwhelmed. Martha was overwhelmed with all the work she did for Jesus's visit while Mary sat and gained wisdom, the woman with the issue of blood was overwhelmed with her condition, Esther was overwhelmed with her duties to her people in the face of the king, and even Jesus was overwhelmed with his destiny to be persecuted and die for the sake of mankind. I felt the pressure of my works for God and my desire to be elevated. I had to be conditioned and pressure washed. I got angry at God because I took over 30 pills twice and still didn't even get sick with vomiting. I felt alone and I was told that I was a fake that my anointing was a joke and that whatever it was I was doing wasn't for God. I was mocked and made fun of, and honestly I couldn't tell if I was just seeing things or if it was truly happening. I didn't understand how God could put so much inside of me but make me so invisible. I was angry and fed up with life. Every day was the same fight, get no sleep, fight with the kids, go to work and be persecuted and beaten down, run around all afternoon in the midst of people with no real sense of compassion, feeling empty and drained I searched for someone to talk to and found no one but those who judged and persecuted me more. At first I prayed and prayed and prayed and prayed some more but after a while I became so tired, so weary and so weak. We should never get weary of doing good says the word of God, but honestly the desire to check off all the boxes God has on your daily to do list is an exhausting task. Love those who are unlovable, forgive those who have hurt you, cancel the debts of those who owe you, be in the world and not of the world, and so on and so on but while the word rings strong in my mind I am still left with this hand full of tears. Still confused as to why some Christians are acting the way they acting towards me when all they preach about on Sunday is love and respect. I'm still hurt because my church family still hasn't used the discernment that God gave them to atone to my spirit to come help me. I am still disappointed that all of my examples of Godly living have become nothing but smoke screens. Lord I am left with all of this garbage but the pick-up day is weeks away. I don't want to pray because I am tired and can't think or sleep, my body is weak from lack of food and my only solace is to end the life that has added 10 years to my face in only two weeks. This is me, the suicidal Christian who knows the word and knows the comings and goings of the spirit realm but still feels the heat of failure upon her neck. But I am not the only one. Lord knows who else feels just like this and the only thing I can do to save my own life is to let go and let God carry me because I am too exhausted to fight this one. The Lord said he put an army around me and all I have to do is give the word. Forgiveness is the hardest part but I am too* tired to hold onto these offenses, cancelling debt seems unfair to me but I am too tired to keep writing these collection notices, my soul is battered and bleeding but I am too tired to keep an eye on the wounds to make sure no one is coming around to pour salt on them. The law of the Lord is surrender and when the sitting of suicide grips your veins, it comes in your exhaustion to fight that God will stand and send the largest army of the heavens to surround you waiting for the word. A gentle whisper and the highest kingdom of the land is there to battle on your behalf while the Lord ministers and mend your heart.

This brief journey through my storm and my battle with suicide is a personal and deeply heart felt one. This is what I lived from start to finish. When I began writing this a couple days ago I was on my second attempt and failure, but as I sat down and finished this in few short hours, I am beginning to feel the strength returning to my body and my blood beginning to pump again. I am beginning to be able to cry out to the Lord in pain in hopes that he hears. For days I couldn't even cry, but today I am at least able to shed the first tear towards release. Yesterday I couldn't even think about going to church and worshipping God, but right now I can at least picture myself in worship once again. The devil is defeated and so with that truth I am able to at least put the pills back in the cabinet and begin to feel like I have a heart that beats for a purpose. Dearly beloved, the only thing I can urge you to do is to first look at those pills before you put them in your mouth because a mere look will begin the journey to reminding you why you are here reading this and how there is more to what you hear in your ears at this moment. I survived because God survived in me and you can survive because I believe in the purpose that was birthed within you. There's beauty in these things of God and you are God's property."

My previous book was written in pain on the cusp of beginning the steps to healing. It wasn't until a recent and final breakdown that I saw my life for what it was and my purpose for what it was manifested to be. As I walked through the journey of this novel, I remembered things that I learned along the way, and I reflected on the things that I have picked up just recently. I have seen the tears of those left behind after suicide, I have heard the screams from hell from the mouths of those remorseful for their decisions. I've seen the faces of strangers that have taken their own lives. Despite whether you think I'm sane or not, the truth is that the state that depression puts a person in is one that can be crippling and debilitating. For a person on the outside, its simple to ask "why?" and to speculate as to where his or her mind was at the time of death; but the fact lays in the truth of what the depressive spirit delivers. The spirit of suicide will manipulate a persons' bad mood, breakup, bad grades, or parents' divorce and turn it into a hopeless and dire situation. The spirit of depression will turn a simple insult into a life altering anxiety attack. Death is a permanent solution to temporary problems and I can say this loud and clear because I have been to the bottom of a pill case, I have been on the sharp end of a razor blade and I have been on the top ledge of the Hudson Bridge. It's easy to imagine what a person goes through, but until you have been there, there is no real absorption of the gutless feeling of fear and no way out. I want to encourage all those who are reading this book. You may look at me differently and some may judge me un-righteously; but my purpose is clear. I am a woman who is saved, sanctified, and filled with the Holy Spirit. I have attempted my life and have almost succeeded. I have heard the cried of heaven when I was too far gone to understand the consequences of my decision. I heard the laughs of the devil when I swallowed enough pills to kill a large man in minutes. I am a walking, breathing, living witness that God does save and God does bring back if you diligently seek him. I want to reach those who have been in this spot and are in this spot. I want those to listen to me who have lost people they cared about to the clutches of self-inflicted death. I want the world to hear me when everything begins to come crashing down around them. There is hope because God is our hope. There is proof that God exists because there is no way that a woman of 160 lbs can take 25 sleeping pills and not have her heart stop. There is a purpose for your life because after all the drugs, alcohol, sex, lies, mistakes, pain that I have caused I still have a purpose. I want you to hear me when I say that yes, the world will judge you, yes, the world will cast you out and make fun of you; but what we endure every day is honorable and is not a defect to our character but a definition to the greatness we have been given. So please, when you are on that ledge, or in that bottle of pills please remember that if I can make it, so can you and I will not let you do it alone because you did not let me do it alone. If you don't think you have any other purpose, your purpose is to keep me pushing this message towards the ears of those who are afraid. Your purpose is to help me help you. And again, with love

The suicidal Christian.

John 14:6

New Living Translation (NLT)

[6] Jesus told him, "I am the way, the truth, and the life. No one can come to the Father except through me.

CHAPTER SEVEN
Encouragement

Through the battle I have discovered that the love of Christ has been my strong suit the entire time. There was a point where I forgot who I was and what I was worth. I found myself cast down and heavy burden with the weight of the world. I awoke each day with grief, grief over the woman that I knew I was and the woman I became in the valley of depression; but I am here, still alive, to encourage you to hold fast to the knowledge of the father. When the fire gets too hot, when the storm gets to dark, when the rain gets too hard, and life gets too bleak; I urge you to hang on and remind yourself of all the promises that the Lord has given you. I have felt hopelessness and I know the impossibility of encouraging yourself in the midst of depression and fear; but I was reminded that I was birthed for a purpose. Even though I didn't see it, I could hear it. I would be at my worst days and the Lord would have someone message me looking for prayer and uplifting; he never failed! I always asked him "why Lord!!??" and I believe that he would smile a bit and then give me the words that would uplift that person but ring true to myself. I was spared by the blood of Jesus. I urge you to seek the Lord and seek after those who you have been gifted with for help. In my sadness I felt alone, like nobody would understand; but I could never escape the smile of friend or family member. I urge you to seek help and to seek an ear because the Lord loves and adores you and he has given you a purpose that rings louder than any lie the enemy could spit into your ear. Remember that I have suffered, I have tried to run, I have tried to give up but here I am. Remember my face because I am a face who survived suicide attempts, I am a face of proof that we all have a reason to exist and that we all can be saved! I love you and you are magnificent!

The Battled Christian

An excerpt from my book *"The Suicidal Christian: the battle is the mind":* "Beloved daughter, beloved daughter, beloved daughter…I see all your pain and I also know who I made you to be and the purpose that is upon your head. I love you and not because I have to but because you are made out of pure diamonds and pearls. Look at me and see that if I didn't love that those pills would have stopped your heart, and destroyed your brain. I watched the devil put the rope around your neck but your purpose is far greater than anything your feeble mind can comprehend while you dwell in the earth of sin. You spend days and nights so upset and frustrated at the sins of others and you question your own salvation when you see the false children of my family are exposed. But look around you Marisa and see the army I have sent to protect you, look and see the fear on the demons faces. Your heart is heavy because of the love you have for me and others. Your hurt because of the trust you put into the worldly church when thee gifts I have given you have given you the ability to see all these secrets on your will. Why be surprised when I sat with you in the night hours and spoke to you about what the next days will bring. How can you doubt the gifts and purposes I have given you when you have seen the souls that your efforts have drawn to me? I don't need you to be perfect to fulfill my works and I don't need you to be anyone or anything else but my beloved daughter in order for me to seek gladness in you. I am God and I am able to handle the sins of the world. I know who has hurt you and I know who you have hurt and my judgment is fair. Your name is in my hand and will never be distorted by the mouths of the wicked. You have my biggest army surrounding you and those who can't see it never knew me and never knew attached to my side for the rib of a man will always return to its original body. You my child are my rib and your desire to come home is the natural desire I have given all man to seek the word and the ways of the kingdom that I have ordained for you. I am your home and I am your light. You are my rib dear child and there is no place in hell for you. There will be no pill to take the life that I have ordained unless I will it so…go forth and continue your works for I am God and I know all. You are my child and I am your father and my love and respect is sufficient for you. I see you dear child and every minute of every breath you take is being monitored by me alone and you will returned home. I love you

CHAPTER EIGHT
What the Bible says about Depression

The Battled Christian

What the Bible says about **Depression**:

Psalm 34:17-18

New Living Translation (NLT)

[17] The LORD hears his people when they call to him for help.
   He rescues them from all their troubles.
[18] The LORD is close to the brokenhearted;
   he rescues those whose spirits are crushed.

Matthew 11:28

New Living Translation (NLT)

[28] Then Jesus said, "Come to me, all of you who are weary and carry heavy burdens, and I will give you rest.

Jeremiah 29:11

New Living Translation (NLT)

[11] For I know the plans I have for you," says the LORD. "They are plans for good and not for disaster, to give you a future and a hope.

1 Peter 5:7

New Living Translation (NLT)

[7] Give all your worries and cares to God, for he cares about you.

Isaiah 41:10

New Living Translation (NLT)

[10] Don't be afraid, for I am with you.
  Don't be discouraged, for I am your God.
I will strengthen you and help you.
  I will hold you up with my victorious right hand.

Psalm 30:5

New Living Translation (NLT)

[5] For his anger lasts only a moment,
  but his favor lasts a lifetime!
Weeping may last through the night,
  but joy comes with the morning.

Proverbs 3:5-6

New Living Translation (NLT)

[5] Trust in the LORD with all your heart;
  do not depend on your own understanding.
[6] Seek his will in all you do,
  and he will show you which path to take.

Psalm 143:7-8

New Living Translation (NLT)

[7] Come quickly, LORD, and answer me,
  for my depression deepens.
Don't turn away from me,
  or I will die.
[8] Let me hear of your unfailing love each morning,
  for I am trusting you.
Show me where to walk,
  for I give myself to you.

The Battled Christian

Romans 12:2

New Living Translation (NLT)

² Don't copy the behavior and customs of this world, but let God transform you into a new person by changing the way you think. Then you will learn to know God's will for you, which is good and pleasing and perfect.

Philippians 4:6-7

New Living Translation (NLT)

⁶ Don't worry about anything; instead, pray about everything. Tell God what you need, and thank him for all he has done. ⁷ Then you will experience God's peace, which exceeds anything we can understand. His peace will guard your hearts and minds as you live in Christ Jesus.

Psalm 9:9

New Living Translation (NLT)

⁹ The LORD is a shelter for the oppressed,
    a refuge in times of trouble.

2 Timothy 1:7

New Living Translation (NLT)

⁷ For God has not given us a spirit of fear and timidity, but of power, love, and self-discipline.

Revelation 21:4

New Living Translation (NLT)

⁴ He will wipe every tear from their eyes, and there will be no more death or sorrow or crying or pain. All these things are gone forever."

Isaiah 40:31

New Living Translation (NLT)

31 But those who trust in the LORD will find new strength.
    They will soar high on wings like eagles.
They will run and not grow weary.
    They will walk and not faint.

Proverbs 12:25

New Living Translation (NLT)

25 Worry weighs a person down;
    an encouraging word cheers a person up.

Isaiah 26:3

New Living Translation (NLT)

3 You will keep in perfect peace
    all who trust in you,
    all whose thoughts are fixed on you!

Romans 15:13

New Living Translation (NLT)

13 I pray that God, the source of hope, will fill you completely with joy and peace because you trust in him. Then you will overflow with confident hope through the power of the Holy Spirit.

The Battled Christian

Psalm 34:18

New Living Translation (NLT)

[18] The LORD is close to the brokenhearted;
  he rescues those whose spirits are crushed.

Philippians 4:13

New Living Translation (NLT)

[13] For I can do everything through Christ who gives me strength.

Deuteronomy 31:8

New Living Translation (NLT)

[8] Do not be afraid or discouraged, for the LORD will personally go ahead of you. He will be with you; he will neither fail you nor abandon you."

Psalm 94:18-19

New Living Translation (NLT)

[18] I cried out, "I am slipping!"
  But your unfailing love, O LORD, supported me.
[19] When doubts filled my mind,
  your comfort gave me renewed hope and cheer.

Mark 5:28

New Living Translation (NLT)

[28] For she thought to herself, "If I can just touch his robe, I will be healed."

Job 7:6-8

New Living Translation (NLT)

6 "My days fly faster than a weaver's shuttle.
   They end without hope.
7 O God, remember that my life is but a breath,
   and I will never again feel happiness.
8 You see me now, but not for long.
   You will look for me, but I will be gone.

Romans 8:28

New Living Translation (NLT)

28 And we know that God causes everything to work together[a] for the good of those who love God and are called according to his purpose for them.

Daniel 4:34

New Living Translation (NLT)

34 "After this time had passed, I, Nebuchadnezzar, looked up to heaven. My sanity returned, and I praised and worshiped the Most High and honored the one who lives forever.

His rule is everlasting,
   and his kingdom is eternal.

2 Samuel 22:2

New Living Translation (NLT)

2 He sang:

"The LORD is my rock, my fortress, and my savior"

The Battled Christian

The Lord says:

"Take heed and harken unto me. I am close to the heavy hearted because it is them that lay down the law and follow me unrestricted. I am the creator of life and the Shepard to the sheep. Even the sickly and the smallest of the few have my eye on them. Darkness was not meant to consume my children and the storm was not meant to drown out my fields. I have placed my right hand on your back and counted all your tears. Your pain is what makes you humble and your wounds are what make your bones strong. When the skin gets cut open, does it not regenerate and form new over the sting? Just like your flesh is designed to do, so is your spirit. So take heed that your hurts now will regenerate into a new life and joy that could have never been achieved without the interruption of the previous path. I am your father and your healer. Look to me and your heart will be renewed."

CHAPTER NINE
What the Bible says about Suicide

The Battled Christian

What the Bible says about **Suicide**:

1 Corinthians 3:16-17

New Living Translation (NLT)

[16] Don't you realize that all of you together are the temple of God and that the Spirit of God lives in[a] you? [17] God will destroy anyone who destroys this temple. For God's temple is holy, and you are that temple.

Ecclesiastes 7:17

New Living Translation (NLT)

[17] On the other hand, don't be too wicked either. Don't be a fool! Why die before your time?

Psalm 34:17-20

New Living Translation (NLT)

[17] The LORD hears his people when they call to him for help.
    He rescues them from all their troubles.
[18] The LORD is close to the brokenhearted;
    he rescues those whose spirits are crushed.

[19] The righteous person faces many troubles,
    but the LORD comes to the rescue each time.
[20] For the LORD protects the bones of the righteous;
    not one of them is broken!

1 Corinthians 6:19-20

New Living Translation (NLT)

[19] Don't you realize that your body is the temple of the Holy Spirit, who lives in you and was given to you by God? You do not belong to yourself, [20] for God bought you with a high price. So you must honour God with your body.

2 Corinthians 12:9

New Living Translation (NLT)

9 Each time he said, "My grace is all you need. My power works best in weakness." So now I am glad to boast about my weaknesses, so that the power of Christ can work through me.

Romans 10:13

New Living Translation (NLT)

13 For "Everyone who calls on the name of the LORD will be saved."[

John 12:25

New Living Translation (NLT)

25 Those who love their life in this world will lose it. Those who care nothing for their life in this world will keep it for eternity.

Psalm 147:3

New Living Translation (NLT)

3 He heals the brokenhearted
and bandages their wounds.

Romans 12:2

New Living Translation (NLT)

2 Don't copy the behavior and customs of this world, but let God transform you into a new person by changing the way you think. Then you will learn to know God's will for you, which is good and pleasing and perfect.

Deuteronomy 30:19

New Living Translation (NLT)

[19] "Today I have given you the choice between life and death, between blessings and curses. Now I call on heaven and earth to witness the choice you make. Oh, that you would choose life, so that you and your descendants might live!

Hebrews 10:35-36

New Living Translation (NLT)

[35] So do not throw away this confident trust in the Lord. Remember the great reward it brings you! [36] Patient endurance is what you need now, so that you will continue to do God's will. Then you will receive all that he has promised

1 Corinthians 3:17

New Living Translation (NLT)

[17] God will destroy anyone who destroys this temple. For God's temple is holy, and you are that temple

Luke 18:1

New Living Translation (NLT)

18 One day Jesus told his disciples a story to show that they should always pray and never give up.

1 Peter 5:6-7

New Living Translation (NLT)

[6] So humble yourselves under the mighty power of God, and at the right time he will lift you up in honor. [7] Give all your worries and cares to God, for he cares about you.

Matthew 6:34

New Living Translation (NLT)

34 "So don't worry about tomorrow, for tomorrow will bring its own worries. Today's trouble is enough for today.

2 Corinthians 4:8-9

New Living Translation (NLT)

8 We are pressed on every side by troubles, but we are not crushed. We are perplexed, but not driven to despair. 9 We are hunted down, but never abandoned by God. We get knocked down, but we are not destroyed.

Psalm 138:7

New Living Translation (NLT)

7 Though I am surrounded by troubles,
   you will protect me from the anger of my enemies.
You reach out your hand,
   and the power of your right hand saves me.

Psalm 118:17

New Living Translation (NLT)

17 I will not die; instead, I will live
   to tell what the LORD has done.

Psalm 139:13

New Living Translation (NLT)

13 You made all the delicate, inner parts of my body
   and knit me together in my mother's womb.

Habakkuk 3:16-19

New Living Translation (NLT)

[16] I trembled inside when I heard this;

my lips quivered with fear.

My legs gave way beneath me,

and I shook in terror.

I will wait quietly for the coming day

when disaster will strike the people who invade us.

[17] Even though the fig trees have no blossoms,

and there are no grapes on the vines;

even though the olive crop fails,

and the fields lie empty and barren;

even though the flocks die in the fields,

and the cattle barns are empty,

[18] yet I will rejoice in the Lord!

I will be joyful in the God of my salvation!

[19] The Sovereign Lord is my strength!

He makes me as surefooted as a deer,

able to tread upon the heights.

The Lord Says:

"The enemy is in the midst and his goal is to convince you that your struggles will end once off my creation. Take heed, the life I have given you is set in the stone of my mind and is carefully watched over by the love of the kingdom that I created. The struggles you endure now are pieces of the eternal puzzle of salvation. Without them the complete picture is impossible. I am a God who knows your ending and it does not include any of the emotions that you're experiencing right now; but includes the glory and the light that I have manifested for you within your mother's womb. You wonder when the pain will end and I urge you to hold onto me. You want to get away from the embarrassment and I unction you to clamp down on my words. There is no shame in the kingdom of God, there is no pain in my presence. Harken unto me and my joy will encompass you, me peace will engulf you, and my healing will surround you. You are not lost and you are not a mistake. You are being watched by the General of the Army that has already won. You are protected and the fire will not consume you. Your pain does have an expiration date and I am the Lord of your reconstruction. Reach up from your pit and hold onto my voice because I am here to pull back my children from the demon of self-infliction."

National Suicide Prevention Lifeline
1-800-273-TALK (8255)
24 hrs. /7 days a week
www.suicidepreventionlifeline.org

References

1. DEPRESSION - DEFINITION AND MORE FROM THE FREE MERRIAM-WEBSTER DICTIONARY. (n.d.). Retrieved December 2013, from http://www.merriam-webster.com/dictionary/depression?show=0&t=1387770078

2. HOW SHOULD A CHRISTIAN DEAL WITH DEPRESSION? WHAT DOES THE BIBLE SAY ABOUT DEPRESSION? (2011). Retrieved 2013, from http://www.compellingtruth.org/Christian-depression.html#ixzz2oGoNZN5h

3. TYPES OF DEPRESSION: MAJOR, CHRONIC, MANIC, AND MORE TYPES. (n.d.). Retrieved 2013, from http://www.webmd.com/depression/guide/depression-types

4. SPIRITUAL WARFARE (2013). Retrieved from a mighty wind: http://www.amightywind.com/whatsnew/090623spiritualwarfare.htm

5. DEPRESSION (MAJOR DEPRESSION): SYMPTOMS - MAYOCLINIC.COM. (n.d.). Retrieved 2013, from http://www.mayoclinic.com/health/depression/DS00175/DSECTION=symptoms

6. Mcclinton, Marisa. THE SUICIDAL CHRISTIAN: THE BATTLE IS THE MIND. 1st ed. highland, ny N.p., 2013. Print.

www.ingramcontent.com/pod-product-compliance
Lightning Source LLC
Chambersburg PA
CBHW081635040426
42449CB00014B/3319